I Went to Hell

By Uebert Angel

Published by: LEVI HOUSE

Unless otherwise stated, all scripture quotations are taken from the King James Version of the Bible.

ISBN 978-1-7399735-0-6

Copyright 2021 by Uebert Angel

Published by LEVI HOUSE

Introduction

I hope you hate what is in this book as much as I do

If you have ever driven behind a semi-truck trailer, you have been warned of the gruesomeness of death and the brevity of life. However, you may not have recognized the warning. It is not written in words but in the form of a low hanging steel bar covered with reflector tape. By law, every semi-truck trailer is required to have one. That bar is a visible reminder of how life can end in an instant. It's called a Mansfield bar for a reason, and it is designed to keep you from following in the footsteps of its namesake.

Jayne Mansfield's spotlight as Hollywood's newest blonde bombshell was beginning to flicker. She had created an image for herself as the naughtier version of the already notorious Marilyn Monroe. Jayne Mansfield was known as much for her tumultuous marriages and love affairs as her risqué behaviour. During a March 1969 interview with BBC, she was asked how much longer she thought she could be a sex symbol. Her answer was prophetic.

"Forever, darling."

Three months later, a couple hours after midnight, a silver 1966 Buick Electra glided down a dark narrow stretch of country road just outside of Louisiana. Mansfield was in the front seat along with the driver and her divorce attorney, who was also her lover. Three of her five children were lying asleep on the back seat. A thick white haze from a city council vehicle spraying the swamps for mosquitoes had settled on the road, cloaking the presence of a slow-moving semi just ahead of them. Before the driver could react, the car ploughed into the back of the truck, and the once quiet night air was filled with the sound of crunching metal and shattered glass.

The Electra slid under the back of the trailer, shearing off the top of the car, taking with it a sizeable piece of the top of Jayne Mansfield's head. Her skull was crushed, sliced open, and forcibly separated from her brain. The grisly scene was a motley of mangled metal, broken bodies, and blood pouring out of what was left of the front of the car.

At just thirty-four years old, Mansfield lived and died by her own words, "If you're going to do something wrong, do it big, because the punishment is the same either way." She lived the fast life and died even faster. There was no time to pray, no time to cry out for mercy, and no time to plead for grace.

Mansfield received numerous marriage proposals during her lifetime, one of them accompanied by a 10-carat diamond ring worth upwards of a quarter of a million dollars at that time. She lived in a 40-room mansion she dubbed as "The Pink Palace." Her life was filled with pomp and grandeur, and she knew she was the embodiment of attraction and, of course, a sex symbol. She was the desire of men and envy of women all over the world. But none of that mattered the moment that car collided with that truck.

Her wish was granted; she would retain her sex symbol status forever. The problem was she was no longer on Earth to lavish in it. She was dead!

You see, you can have all the trappings of life, money in the bank, fine cars, beautiful houses, the best of everything and everyone screaming your name. But if you fail to realize that there is more to life than what you see and experience here on Earth, you are foolish. Life can be very short and death abrupt, and according to the Bible, to neglect your soul is stupidity gone on rampage.

In all my life, I have never seen a moving truck following a hearse. In other words, whatever physical possessions you acquire, when you leave this earth, you will not carry any of them with you. Ladies and gentlemen, when Heaven calls, and Hell calls, you will answer whether you like it or not. Every one of us will live forever. The question is, where?

WHY I WROTE THIS BOOK

Of all the books I have written, I hated writing this one the most. I did not want to write it. However, the love of God compels me to do it. So, here is a book with a reality of the things I have seen beyond the curtain of time. And these words that describe what my eyes saw came to me and demanded to be spoken. I consider myself to be a strong person, but there are some experiences that confront the limits of your physicality. Recalling my visitation of Hell is one of them.

Telling you some of what I saw in Hell requires me to relive the experience and vividly recall sounds, sights, and smells that I wish I could forget. I am reliving what it is like to be in Hell in hopes that you will never live there.

Some believe Hell is somewhere out there in the void; others go as far as to say that Earth is Hell. There are even people who believe that there is no Heaven or Hell, and this earthly experience is all there is. But they are sorely mistaken. If they are sincere in these assumptions, then they are sincerely wrong. I'm here to tell you that there is a world beyond this. Just as Heaven is real, Hell is also real. I saw it. It is not out there somewhere or something that will appear at some time in the distant future. Hell exists right now, and the Bible is not silent about it.

Let me point out that what I am about to share with you is not anything that I watched on a movie screen or was simply told about. I was there. And everything that I share with you in this book is real. Not only that, but the experiences I witnessed in Hell are still happening right now.

My prayer is that you will not approach this book as if it is some fairy tale or work of fiction designed to entertain you. This book is your Mansfield bar. It is here to make you aware of the reality of Hell that awaits those who do not receive the Lord Jesus as their Savior.

What I'm about to tell you is not theory or something I've heard someone else talk about. I am about to share with you my firsthand account of *some* of what I saw in Hell. I repeat, *some of what I saw*, not all there is, but just *some*. As incredible as it will read, what I have revealed on the pages of this book barely scratches the surface of the horrors of Hell. Remember, this is your "Mansfield bar," so don't take this book lightly. Your life depends on it.

Chapter 1

An Unexpected Journey

"**WELCOME TO HELL**." The imposing ominous words were carved deep into either side of the immense gate in bold letters that seemed to be made from a form of medieval wrought iron. The first word, "**WELCOME**," was etched on the left door of the gate. Then, to provide a clue that this was no ordinary destination, the last two words, "**TO HELL**," were positioned slightly lower on the other door on the right side of the gate. The symmetry of the juxtaposed words was meticulous, as if to welcome the condemned with diabolic grandeur, or perhaps so the angels in flight might gaze on them in awe. It was an extraordinary sight to behold. This was a destination like no other, possessing an atmosphere to match and horrors to terrify even the bravest of men.

The benighted live looking hinges of each door of the gate glistened with a material that was reminiscent of the deep saturated hue of lapis lazuli, giving them the façade of polished jewels. At their opening, alternating rows of bas-relief creatures unbeknown to our world formed the processional way. Their faces were a mixture of creatures extinct in our mortal world. Something on them suggested fear just by the sheer look of them. I was spellbound by the complete tenseness of the atmosphere, because inside the horrors of what I was seeing, the brilliance of the designer of that place was evident in everything. Now, whether I was in the flesh or in the spirit, I will not say. But, one thing was sure, I was now in Hell – the home of the condemned.

The Day It All Happened

It all happened at our first house in Great Britain on a street called High Peak Road, in Ashton-Under-Lyne, six miles from the bustling city of Manchester. I was in my bedroom, intending to go to bed. As is always the case with God's visitations with me, I was not expecting anything to happen any more than I expected to be the first person to land on the moon. All of a sudden, the walls began to disappear before my very eyes, starting with the bedroom walls. As I stood there, I watched as, one by one, each wall folded down and away from me, like an envelope being unfolded by a force unknown and unseen. I had experienced this many times before, so I knew exactly what was happening. A *mara* - an open vision - was taking place. The Lord was in the house. I could feel Him all over. The inanimate walls and furniture in my bedroom seemed to have noticed it long before I did.

I had just finished praying right there in my room. And in what felt like a fraction of a second, the atmosphere was transformed. If it were possible, you could slice the atmosphere with a knife. It was that thick. A blanket of rows of a white substance, like patches of altocumulus undulatus clouds, filled the room. As I looked, I could see each row of these cloud-like objects winding and folding into each other. Then as suddenly and unexpectedly as the clouds had appeared, it happened. As I stood in the middle of that wonder, my eyes were opened to what looked like the edges of a box-like transport made of shafts of light.

The Transport to Hell

It was a solid but fluffy looking contraption. I am trying to describe wonders that we mortals could never comprehend naturally. I cannot call it an elevator. To call it an elevator would lower the ingenuity in this holy technological advancement. An escalator would not even come close. However, this was not something new to me. I had seen something like it before, slightly different but the same mechanism, so I knew what it was. It was close in form to the one I had seen in one of my visitations with the Lord.

With no audible beckoning, a force from within made me approach the entrance of the transport. As I approached, the cloud-like substance began to dissipate as if welcoming me aboard. There, standing by the door of the transport, was a huge angelic being waiting to escort me to the spirit world.

I recognized the angel as one who had escorted me to Heaven before, so when I saw him, I was flooded with peace. I immediately thought, *we are going to Heaven*. You see, I had the erroneous idea that this was one of the many trips to Heaven the Lord had promised me months prior to this visitation. So you can imagine my surprise when, after boarding the transport, instead of going up to Heaven as in times before, we started going down.

The vehicle travelled at a phenomenal speed as it made its descent, faster than any speed the human mind can comprehend. I grabbed my stomach instinctively as if the natural world and its contents could have churned in protest. However, the direction was not a deterrent since I felt Heaven could be anywhere and any direction could take me there. You see, whenever the Lord would allow me to peer through the curtain of time and visit Heaven, we always travelled up. But now, we were on a fast trajectory down. I began to think that maybe God was going to show me some other places that are under what we call Heaven. I was in for a surprise.

As we neared our destination, and the transportation contraption began to slow to a stop, I could see creatures moving near the base of it. These were not earthly creatures, but some of them were shaped like dogs, some were like monkeys. Others of humanoid form moved at snap speeds so fast, their blurred images made it difficult to identify what they were.

I looked at the angelic being. And without opening his mouth, he uttered two words that impacted me so much, as if he had spoken a billion words.

"Fear not."

The box-like transport made of shafts of light came to a sudden halt in the most spectacular and effortless soft landing. As the door opened, light flooded in. A short distance away, I could make out gate-like features protruding from more forms of altocumulus undulatus clouds. This time they were thicker than before and whiter than the purest white you could imagine. I must remind you that I am describing spiritual things, which is harder than trying to describe ice to a hermit. So, bear with me.

Entering Hell

As we exited the contraption and walked closer to the gates, the clouds dissipated in a rhythmic way, just as they had done before as I approached the transport. Glory smoke was all around us, and again, I thought I was in Heaven. Then with a resounding thud, the gates swung ajar, and I saw it, an enormous monstrosity with the grandest material form. It was not as big as Heaven's gate, but it was monumental, nonetheless.

The gates were coated in white but dark black within, and there was brilliant white smoke billowing out from it. Once more, I had the thought that this was a region of Heaven. But as we approached the gate, I looked at the edge of the right side of it, and there written in big, bold letters was the location, "... **TO HELL**."

On the left side, just above it, there were other words that I could not make out at first. But as I looked on, the smoke cleared, and I could see the entire message clearly. "**WELCOME TO HELL**." I was confused. *Why would Hell have a welcome sign?* The angel who was with me answered my thoughts.

"Your questions will be answered here."

After you hear of my visitation, prayerfully align yourself to God's perfect will for your life. You do not want to end up

11

there. You will not even wish your worst enemy such evil as I saw in Hell. The things I witnessed are difficult to communicate. Still, it is paramount that I explain, though it is not possible to fully describe all that I saw. So, bear with me as I explain the inexplicable and take you on a tour of Hell.

Chapter 2

BEYOND THE GATE OF HELL

We moved closer to the gate, and as if it could sense our presence, it opened of its own accord. As soon as the gate opened, I was overwhelmed by the pungent, putrid stench of rotting flesh. I knew it was the smell of human flesh, although I had not seen or experienced any human flesh on Earth that smelled anything like it. I don't know how I knew, but somehow, I just knew it was human flesh. And I was thinking, flesh should be left on Earth when the dead depart. But here I was in Hell smelling the pungent, putrid stench of human corpses mixed with char and other chemicals our science community is yet to discover.

Understand that when someone dies on Earth, the body immediately begins to decompose and emits distinct odours. The stench of a decomposing body is compared to rotting fruit combined with the sharp foul smell of stale urine and faecal matter. It is a rank and pungent smell mixed with a tinge of sickening sweetness, like a drop of cheap perfume on a piece of rotting meat that has been left in the hottest sun for days. Imagine a million rotting rats around you, a reeking malodour of the highest degree that would make you gag from five thousand kilometers away, and you would not even be scratching the surface of what Hell smells like.

The smell of Hell alone is a quadrillion times worse than anything you have ever experienced and will ever experience put together. It is an odour that is so radioactive and virulent that if it leaked to Earth, every life—plant, animal, human and otherwise—would die in milli-seconds. As a matter of fact, if the smell was all there is in Hell, you would not wish your worst foe to be there or to experience it for even a second as punishment. It is, simply put, unbearable!

When a body begins to decompose in a house, it can take years for the smell to leave. It lingers in the background, saturating the very fibres of everything around it. The bacteria from the corpse clings to the hair in your nostrils and remultiplies so that you can still smell it even after being away from it for hours. But this pales in comparison to the smell of Hell.

In Hell, the smell of rotting flesh is indescribable. The smell of death—decomposed bodies, burning flesh, and all things rotten and unclean—multiplies and intensifies ad infinitum. Every evil and foul smell you could imagine on Earth combined would smell like the sweetest perfume compared to the smell of Hell.

It was an all-out assault on my senses, penetrating beyond just the olfactory. The smell got into my throat and coated my taste buds. It caused my eyes to weep. It permeated every pore, crawled under my skin, pierced through my bones, and saturated every cell in the marrow. It was alive and menacingly cruel. It was a smell that caused me to wretch and perspire with nausea. And each bead of sweat blanketed my skin with the same fetid stench from which I wanted to escape. If Hell were just the smell alone, I would not wish my worst enemy to be there.

As I struggled to comprehend the stench of Hell, I realised that something greater had overpowered my being. I suddenly had the strength of something indescribable and a certain peace I had not felt before. The place I was standing became holy, yet I was in Hell. Within minutes of arriving, I had gone from fear to awe and now peace, and I could not understand why.

As I regained my bearings, there in front of me was the reason why suddenly, I was at peace. With a radiance that I can only describe as 'liquid love', was The Lord Jesus Christ Himself, standing right in front of me. Mesmerised by Him, I actually forgot the location I was in for a moment, until he beckoned for me to look in a certain direction. In His usual manner (from my past visitations with Him), there was no greeting, small talk or the formalities you and I observe when we meet each other. It was straight to the business at hand. God already knows how you're doing; in fact, he knows how you're doing better than you do yourself! I looked around, thinking I was going to see a big tower and a pit. Then the Lord pointed towards an area that was about 200 meters from the gate where we entered. What I saw was not one big pit, as I expected. Instead, there were a lot of pits in the ground, multiple holes of varying sizes. There was one big one and one that was relatively big compared to that one, but not as large. Some of the pits were very small with small openings.

I asked the Lord, "Shouldn't there be one big hole or pit?"

His response caught me off guard. "Hell is a living organism. It is something with a belly, with legs, with a head, with walls, and even with jaws." He continued. "Remember in My word that I've said that Hell is simply temporal."

15

I was taken aback. What He was saying had not occurred to me. As a matter of fact, I had no recollection of it until He added, "For Hell shall be thrown into the Lake of fire. Have you not wondered why Hell should be punished?"

Then I remembered Isaiah 5:14 which says:

"Therefore hell hath enlarged herself, and opened her mouth without measure: and their glory, and their multitude, and their pomp, and he that rejoiceth, shall descend into it."

Another scripture came rushing in, which was Isaiah 14:15:

"Yet thou shalt be brought down to hell, to the sides of the pit."

As I reflected on the Lord's words and the scriptures that rushed in, something else caught my eye. There were two massive trees. These were the only greenish things I saw in thatarea. Everywhere else looked like a desert with sand dunes that were brownish in colour, as though they had been scorched or charred from the unbearable heat of the atmosphere of hell. As I continued to survey the charred terrain, I came near to one of the pits in the ground and looked down one of the small openings. It was not what I saw that sent chills down my spine, but what I could not see.

Chapter 3

Alone In The Dark

Inside the hole was pitch-black darkness that was tangible, palpable. This was more than the absorption of light like the Black Hole of the earthly universe. This was the very absence of light. The blackness was so dense that you could not sense your hand in front of your face, much less see it.

It was more than just being pitch-black. The darkness had texture, a feeling to it. It emanated an ominous, sinister presence like being surrounded by an impenetrable curtain of blackness and waiting for the next nefarious attack to strike from within it.

When you are at home, you might quickly turn on the light when you enter a room for fear of what you think may be lurking in the darkness. But the darkness in Hell does not cloak a possible or probable threat, but a guaranteed attack that can come at any given moment. The darkness heightens the sense of panic because there is no clue which direction that attack will come from or what form it will take.

Imagine for a moment that you are in a pitch-black hole of Hell, no light whatsoever. You feel around, but there is nothing for you to grab a hold of, no way for you to anchor yourself in the pitch-black space. Fear creeps down your body from the top of your head to the soles of your feet.

What you feel is not goosebumps. It is the frantic searching of your brain firing signals to every nerve ending in your body in a desperate attempt to reorient itself to its environment. It is shooting blind, failing to identify cause or effect. The lack of visual stimuli causes your brain to malfunction. It can no longer differentiate what is real from what is not. The only feeling it can identify is sheer and absolute terror. That is the only signal broadcast through your nervous system in an infinite loop.

You cannot see or feel anything solid beneath you, and you can no longer tell if you are moving forward or backwards, falling or standing. You are overwhelmed and disoriented completely. Your fight or flight response is in a state of utter chaos as anarchy prevails over your sympathetic nervous system. Fear is excreting from every orifice of your body, and perspiration streams from every pore. But instead of cooling your body down, you feel hot, like a hyperpyrexic fever that will never break.

Your heart is racing. You try to clutch your chest, but you can no longer tell where your body is. Your spirit, soul, and body feel displaced. Your mouth salivates as wave after unending wave of nausea turns your stomach into an open cavity hurling its acids up into the back of your throat and through your nose and mouth. A gurgled scream manages to escape, but it hits the impenetrable wall of blackness and is swallowed up. You are in the darkness of Hell.

As we went closer, there was a sense of profound loneliness. I was there as an observer. Still, I was given an awareness of my surroundings. I knew intuitively that there were a lot of people there. At the same time, I knew that

Hell is a lonely place where each occupant is encapsulated in eternal solitary confinement.

Isolation is its own torment. Any prisoner of war that has spent time in isolation can tell you that. Under abnormal circumstances on Earth, extreme isolation is proven to have severe negative psychological effects, including anxiety, panic attacks, and paranoia. Add to that the lack of sleep, and you have conditions that are ripe for psychosis, hallucinations, and overall mental breakdown. But that is a walk in the park compared to Hell's effect on the human psyche.

Imagine being confined to a small cell with no human interaction, engulfed in pitch-blackness, not for days or weeks, but for a timeless eternity. You are in black darkness, but you can never sleep. Hell creates an environment that is the direct antithesis to the social beings humans are designed to be. It is the ultimate social distancing, pushing its inhabitants to the verge of insanity, but never kind enough to allow them to lose their minds. There are no hallucinations in Hell. The never-ending nightmares are real, and the nightmares don't just happen at night but also during the day, but all is darkness; even the day is pitch black.

As I pondered on the darkness in Hell, the Lord opened my eyes to see the horrors of Hell through the pitch-dark blackness, and my ears were opened to hear the wailing and groanings of its tormented captives. As I looked through the darkness, the first thing I noticed was the effects of Hell's suffocating atmosphere. There was no oxygen to breathe normally.

Suffocating in Hell

I watched as the occupants went for indefinite periods without oxygen as if they were being strangled, a sense of panic gripping them as their lungs were robbed of air. They wanted to breathe and were making every effort, but nothing was happening. They remained in that condition for long periods, crying and gasping for air that did not exist. And since there is no time in Hell, each moment seemed like an eternity.

Just when they reached a point where it looked like they would find relief in death, a wisp of oxygen or a wisp of life would be made available. They would take a sharp, very brief inhalation of air or life, just enough to keep them alive. Then the oxygen, or whatever it is that sustained them there, would disappear, and the suffocation would start all over again. They remained in that vicious cycle, staying on the verge of one of the worst possible ways to die but never being able to die. It was like dying over and over again, forever. I don't know the composition of their new bodies, but they looked almost the same as their earthly bodies that had been left to rot on Earth. Their new bodies could feel pain at a more than astronomical level. They could smell, burn, rot and still be sustained in this ecosystem of Hell.

This is just the beginning of our tour, and I am only describing the parts I saw. Hell is filled with unspeakable atrocities that make the most heinous crimes on Earth look like mere child's play. What I saw next is emblazoned in the deepest recesses of my mind. Never in your wildest dreams could you imagine a sight like what I'm about to show you. It was brilliant, but in the worst way possible.

Chapter 4

The Ring of Fire

I observed that Hell has its own customization system. The flesh of the humans I saw there was in a recreated form. It looked like the body they died with, but it was a new body designed specifically to be used as an instrument of torture. I did not see a raging inferno in which all of the occupants of Hell were burning. What I saw was much more terrifying than that. There was fire, but this was a bespoke fire, tailored for each occupant. Each person had their own personal inferno and a body custom-crafted to experience the full effect of it.

There is no way to fully describe in earthly terms the things I saw in Hell. I am relating what I saw and offering information in language you can understand. But there is no true comparison between the things on Earth and the things I witnessed in Hell. Hell is a supernatural yet physical place, and though I may use familiar terms, you must take into account that everything in Hell is experienced at a heightened level, a billion times more intense than anything on Earth.

Here on Earth, there are different kinds of flames with varying degrees of heat. When you see a bonfire or campfire, you may not have thought about what it is showing you by virtue of its colour. All fire is hot, but all fire is not the same.

Fire has colours that vary from the innermost part of the flame to the outermost. The dominant colour in a flame changes with temperature, the innermost being the hottest. In other words, the further you get from the centre of the flame, the lower the temperature will be.

For example, when you look at a fire in a wood-burning fireplace, the temperature colour range of the flames is from red (outermost) to yellow or white (innermost). The hottest colour possible for organic material such as wood is yellow. Above the yellow region, the colour changes to orange, which is cooler, then red, which is cooler still.

Each colour has a spectrum of varying degrees of heat. A red flame that is just visible starts at around 525 °C (980 °F) and gets to a cherrycoloured clear as hot as 1,000 °C (1,800 °F). A white flame starts at around 1,300 to 1,400 °C (2,400 °F) and gets to a dazzling whitehot at 1,600 °C (2,900 °F). Any time you see a blue flame, it is hotter than white, a searing 1,650 °C (3,000 °F). But we have found ways to make the blue flame even hotter by combining gases.

Gas burns hotter than wood. The hottest fires produced by oxyacetylene welding torches combine oxygen and gas to create pinpoint blue flames that burn upwards of a blistering 3,000 to 3,300 degrees °C (6,000 °F). At those temperatures, you can cut through steel like butter. Several years ago, scientists discovered that at the Earth's core, it is 6,000 °C (approximately 11,000 °F). Hell is at the centre of the Earth, which is why if you die and go to Hell, no matter where you are on the planet, you will always go down.

I need you to understand that what I saw in Hell was not natural fire. It was a supernatural fire that burned hotter than anything on Earth. This was not an external fire that started somewhere and then engulfed the person all at once, no. This was an inside job.

I watched in horror as the blistering hot flame started from the inside of the person's body and moved like a fine-tuned instrument in a way that maximized all of its destructive capabilities. This fire did not rush. It was a liquid blue flame that crept with calculating precision as if in slow motion, millimetre by millimetre, starting at the soles of the feet.

First, the skin cracked, and the nerve endings all fired at the same time. As the unrelenting flame continued its path of consumption, the hair was singed. Next, the body heated up from the fire, and the fat underneath the skin began to melt. As the fat melted, the skin began to slough off and fall away in flakes and sheets. The fire was relentless and focused, burning and eating away in one location until all the remaining flesh was thoroughly consumed. Only then did it inch its way up to the next part of the body.

Once the skin and surface tissue melted and burned away, the underlying tissue and muscle were the next to cook, then burn. As the fire traversed upwards, the internal organs heated to the boiling point, then exploded. And as the muscles were consumed by the fire, they too dried up, withered, and burned away, leaving enough of the skeletal frame behind to serve as the scaffold for the fire's continued climb.

By the time it reached the face, it burned through tissue and muscle. When it got to the eyes, the eyelids and thin tissue were destroyed, and the eyeballs boiled, then burst, and finally burned. The brain, scalp, and the hair on the head were the last to be consumed. Once the fire got to the very top of the head, the body recreated itself from the bottom up, and the fire started all over again from the soles of the feet.

My eyes were fastened to the horrific sight before me. In spite of my awareness that this was a place of torment, my soul was overwhelmed with perturbation. I took issue with seeing these tortured souls in such excruciating pain. *What could they possibly have done to deserve such torment?*

I turned to the Lord for answers to the unsettling questions in my heart.

"Lord, why are they burning?"

He remained quiet, which only added to my angst. Then, as if by silent delegation, the angel who was with me responded.

"They failed to receive the free gift of Jesus."

His words hung in the atmosphere like a dark storm cloud about to erupt. I turned them over in my mind.

Knowing my consternation, the angel continued. "The Lord changes hearts, not actions."

This time, my tone was more subdued than before. "I do not understand."

With an air of finality, the angel responded once more. "Changed hearts change actions, but changed actions do not change hearts."

The cloud rolled away from my heart as my understanding was enlightened. These souls were burning, but it was not about anything they had done. It was not about their actions at all. It was about the inactivity of their heart. *They failed to receive the free gift of Jesus.* In doing so, they had rejected the only One who could change their hearts. Therefore, their hearts could never be changed. Consequently, their actions could never be changed. They had sentenced themselves to an unending cycle of torment. Change was no longer possible.

I returned my attention to the tortured souls before me. As the fiery cycle of pain continued, there was no unconscious moment to provide relief. This was no earthly fire. It could not be cooled, smothered, starved, or doused. This was Hellfire. The person felt everything with supernaturally heightened awareness, and they were caught in an endless loop of inextinguishable eternal flame.

The Lord had a lot to say about Hell when He was here on Earth in the flesh. There are over 162 references in the New Testament alone that warn of Hell. And over 70 of these references were uttered by the Lord Jesus Christ. You see, there is a real hot fire in Hell. In Luke 16:22-28, Jesus Christ gives a frightening picture of what is there:

"The rich man also died, and was buried; and in hell he lift up his eyes, being in torments, and saw Abraham afar off, and Lazarus in his bosom. And he cried and said, Father Abraham, have mercy on me, and send Lazarus, that he may dip the tip of his finger in water, and cool my tongue; for I am tormented in this flame. But Abraham said, Son, remember that thou in thy lifetime received good things,

and likewise Lazarus evil things: but now he is comforted, and thou art tormented. And beside all this, between us and you there is a great gulf fixed: so that they which would pass from hence to you cannot; neither can they pass to us, that would come from thence. Then he said, I pray thee therefore, Father, that Thou would send him to my father's house: For I have five brethren; that he may testify unto them, lest they also come into this place of torment."

Here are a few other passages that speak of the fires of Hell:

The man in Luke 16:24 cries: "... **I am tormented in this FLAME.**"

Then in Matthew 13:42, Jesus says:

"**And shall cast them into a FURNACE OF FIRE: there shall be wailing and gnashing of teeth.**"

In Matthew 25:41, Jesus says:

"**... Depart from me, ye cursed, into everlasting FIRE ...**"

And Revelation 20:15 says:

"**And whosoever was not found written in the book of life was cast into the LAKE OF FIRE.**"

Everyone in Hell burns the way they deserve. No one burning there will ever say there is an issue that they shouldn't burn for or say they weren't invited. Hell is real, and you can be a candidate.

As I looked on and contemplated what the angel of the Lord had revealed to me, I perceived that Hell is a place of perfection, perfected pain and punishment. It was the flip side of Heaven. I was standing in an environment of ultimate equal opportunity, a destination of destruction. This institution upheld a policy of inclusion and will never post a "No Vacancy" sign.

Anyone is welcome, regardless of their socioeconomic status, race, or creed, whether male, female, or nonbinary. Hell welcomes them all with greedy urgency. It is a perversion of the invitation to "come as you are." And I was being given a shocking glimpse of some of the people who had accepted that invitation. As we continue this tour, so will you.

The next thing I saw was so gutwrenching that I considered not including it in this book. However, I was given a mandate to speak on these things and warn of the soon return of the King.

Chapter 5

The Suffocating Power of Hell

There is only one thing as jarring as the frenzied tumult of Hell, and that is the deafening silence. Hell is so noisy and chaotic that when you enter an area where there is silence, the silence itself rushes into your ears like a roar. I will never forget one of those occasions during my tour. It was like watching a mime acting out a macabre scene. Sadly, this was no act. It was real.

The Lord had opened my eyes to see through the pitch-black darkness. It was a surreal experience, much like seeing an intense beam of light projecting directly onto a singular spot on a black stage. I saw the light and could see clearly, but the tortured captive remained in, and sensed only, darkness.

He was writhing in pain, clutching at his throat. He was thrashing his head wildly from side to side, searching frantically for help that would never come. The raised veins in his neck looked as though the blood were about to burst through at any moment. His eyes began to bulge and protrude, barely hanging on from the sockets. His mouth gaped open, contorted and stretched beyond human capacity. His parched tongue was tearing away at the frenulum as if it were trying to escape from his mouth. His lips, tongue, face, and hands were now a greyish purplish-blue. He was dying.

He wanted to scream, but he could not. He could not make a sound because there was no oxygen to produce it. His heart raced in a vain effort to push blood to the brain as his airways began to fill with brackish foam.

Although he could not speak, tears streamed down the man's face only to quickly evaporate in the torrid atmosphere. Not even tears could provide relief in Hell. Because of the heightened sensitivity of his supernatural flesh-like body, he could feel the cells in his brain dying, like nuclear explosions in his head. He wished to succumb to unconsciousness, even to die, anything to stop the pain. But the only wish that is granted in Hell is your choice to be there. And this was only a restart of a never-ending cycle of dying.

His mind and failing bodily systems tell him that he is dying. Too weak to clutch at his throat anymore, his arms loll at his sides. His heart stammers painfully in his chest. He feels he is at the very brink of death, but he remains in that state for what seems like an eternity, dying but never dying.

I squirmed uncomfortably at the scene before me. I could not bear this sight – it was too horrific for an apt description. I wanted it to end, but there seemed to be no end in sight. Suddenly, a wisp appears near his face, like a small cloud of white smoke. What remains of his body reacts instinctively, and he takes a sharp, brief inhalation of air. It is just enough to bring him back to life. I had not realized how tense the scene in front of me had caused my body to become. But as signs of life began to reappear, I could feel the muscles in my body began to relax a little.

The angel turned to me. The sound of his voice piercing the silence startled me, and my head snapped around to look at him. "Look." He directed my attention back to the dying man. "This is not the oxygen that keeps them alive. It's God's permitted life."

My relief for the dying man was short-lived because the cycle of suffocation had started all over again. You would think that the wisp of air would provide temporary relief from the suffering. It does not. It actually adds to it. As the oxygen is expelled, the man clutches again at his throat. The brain cells explode. The bluish discolouration reappears. The lungs begin to rupture. The body begins to swell. And the cycle of suffocation repeats all over again.

Suffocation is one of the worst possible ways to die. But imagine suffocating – not just in feeling but in actuality – yet never being able to die. In Hell you can be suffocating every moment. And since there is no time in Hell, each moment feels like an eternity. You teeter at the precipice of death, only to be brought back to life so you can experience dying over and over and over again, ad infinitum. Such is the nature of Hell.

I mentioned earlier how Hell does not discriminate. Anyone from any social stratification can be there, people from all walks of life, from church folk to the world's most notorious killers. What I was allowed to see next proved this sad reality.

Chapter 6

Come As You Are

From where I was standing, the Lord said, "Look there." And I looked toward the gate where we had come in. As I looked on, the gate opened, and I saw four angels with their arms outstretched, each holding the other's hand to form an angelic guard or barrier, as it were. There were four other angels linked in a similar fashion who were standing behind masses of people, moving them forward as they guided them through the gates of Hell. The moment one group of angels corralled a group of Hell's invitees inside, they joined the line and moved to the rear to bring the next group of clueless victims in.

I was perplexed at the sight of the angels. Being the inquisitive person I am, I asked the Lord a question.

"Why are there angels there?"

His eyes remained fixed on the scene in front of us. "To come to this place, you are guarded so that you don't go any other way except here."

I paused for a moment recollecting my previous visitations to Heaven. In Heaven, there were no angelic guards to guide you in. The pearly gates open, and you enter. I questioned the Lord further.

"Why is it so serious that you need to be guarded?"

His eyes moistened. "Because I give you the desires of your heart. The moment you did not choose Me on Earth, you decided that your desire is Hell, and I'm fulfilling that desire."

Crimes in Hell

In Heaven, you are known as you were known on Earth. In Hell, you are also known as you were known. If you used to hate when you were on Earth, you continue to hate in Hell. The only difference is there are no restrictions or limitations to that hatred. Whatever malevolent intent you harboured in your heart before you died remains and proliferates without restraint. That was a lesson I learned while in Hell, and it was not taught by instruction but by observation.

I saw rape being committed in Hell that would make the most egregious and perverse cases on Earth seem humane. I witnessed murders happening in Hell that would make the likes of Jeffrey Dahmer, Ted Bundy, and Jack the Ripper seem as saintly as Mother Theresa.

I know what I'm telling you might be confusing because you're wondering if you die in Hell. No, you do not die; you cannot. But you can experience dying and death over and over. One thing is certain, everything you used to do here on Earth, you will continue doing in Hell. A robber will still be attempting to rob only in a more heightened sense. A rapist will still rape, but at a higher magnitude. A murderer will still try to kill but in the most atrocious way. In Hell, everything is heightened to the highest degree because you are in the spiritual realm.

Hell is a place of renewal. Evil never expires. On Earth, you can suffer, but you can have the hope of death to escape that suffering. But in Hell, the suffering never ends; it is renewed continually, a perpetual torment, and you can never die or escape.

I vividly recall seeing a woman trying to escape from one of the pits. It was like a horrific scene from Nightmare on Elm Street but a million times worse. I watched this woman as she tried to climb out. There was something like a rail at the edge of the pit that she grabbed and started to pull herself up. I can only imagine how she must have felt as she gripped the rail - the combined feeling of desperation and terror mingled with hope at the possibility of escape. I felt she was just about to make it out of the pit. One more pull and she would have been out. Just as she was about to heave herself out, a spirit being with razor-sharp claws about half a meter long - nearly 2-feet - plunged its claws straight into her back and dragged her back down into the pit.

I was so shocked, I turned to the Lord. "Is that a demon?"

The angelic being that was with us chimed in. "There are no demons in this place. Their time is coming, but this is not the time."

Right then, as if on cue, verses came to me. One in particular, from Matthew 8:29, stuck in my mind:

"And, behold, they cried out, saying, What have we to do with thee, Jesus, thou Son of God? Art thou come hither to torment us before the time?"

I knew then that demons will have a specific time to reach this place, but as of the moment I was there, that time had not yet come.

The angel continued, "Do you not know that this place is not prepared for you who have received Christ? This is a place for the condemned, not for the saved."

The Lord quickly took over and uttered words that were familiar to me. "I have said in My Word, there is therefore now no condemnation to them which are in Christ Jesus, who walk not after the flesh, but after the Spirit. For the law of the Spirit of life in Christ Jesus hath made me free from the law of sin and death. For what the law could not do, in that it was weak through the flesh, God sending His own Son in the likeness of sinful flesh, and for sin, condemned sin in the flesh: That the righteousness of the law might be fulfilled in us, who walk not after the flesh, but after the Spirit. For they that are after the flesh do mind the things of the flesh; but they that are after the Spirit the things of the Spirit. For to be carnally minded is death; but to be spiritually minded is life and peace. Because the carnal mind is enmity against God: for it is not subject to the law of God, neither indeed can be. So then, they that are in the flesh cannot please God."

I knew this was word for word Apostle Paul's epistle to the Romans, and to be exact chapter 8:1-8. I also knew that in verse 9 of the same chapter, it goes on to say:

"**But ye are not in the flesh ...**"

That showed me the Lord never intended for us to be in that location, but people choose to end up there by their own volition. I understood that to be there was an act of one's own choice; no one forced them to be there. I also knew that when you end up there, you cannot escape even if you wanted to. There are no emergency exits!

Hell has no escape route. You will try to escape to no avail. It is a place managed by spirit beings inside through a force that controls the universe. You will not wander around and end up in a safe location. No, there is no provision for a break. It's all-time suffering and burning. Hell is not a nice place. And even if you somehow managed to get out, which is impossible, angels are guarding the outside. No one escapes, spirit or human. There is no way to escape once you are in Hell. You are allowed to hope only to have that hope snatched away from you in the most excruciating ways imaginable. Hope and faith there are useless commodities. They won't get you out, and no matter how you try to repent, you won't get forgiveness that can change your location.

Hell is a place of utter chaos and unspeakable violence, where victimizers prey upon one another in a continuous vicious cycle. The vilest criminals, the most sadistic killers, and the most depraved sexual deviants victimizing and being victimized with no chance of remorse, repentance, or relief.

Chapter 7

The Holding Cell

The sound of Hell is like no other. As the inhabitants were forced beyond the threshold of pain and suffering, I was engulfed in a deafening cacophony of shrieks, wailing, deep guttural cries, moans, and other unidentifiable sounds. Obscenities streamed from the lips of the unrepentant as they demanded to be released from this place of anguish. Every inhabitant had entered the same way, through the infamous and immense gates of Hell. But once inside, there were no random places of assignment. Instead, everyone had a designated place of confinement.

It was organized chaos. And as we moved from one stop of the gruesome tour to the next, everyone was in their place. Each person was receiving their due punishment based on the severity of their crimes and misconduct on Earth. Everywhere I looked, there was agony. Had it not been for the strengthening I received, I would not have been able to endure it. Still, I was deeply troubled by what I saw.

"Why are they here?" It was as much a plea of my heart as a question.

The angel of the Lord replied. "It is like a remand before the final sentence."

I searched the database of my mind to draw on my legal knowledge in an attempt to grasp what the angel said. *It was like a remand.*

The angel continued. "They know why they are here, but the judgment has not been set."

You see, on Earth, a remand is issued if the court believes the accused is a flight risk. The defendant has already been found guilty, but they are placed in a holding cell until final sentencing can be carried out on judgment day. That is why the angel said, "judgment has not been set." The thought of these pitiful inhabitants being flight risks made me shudder as I recalled the woman trying to climb out of the pit. They would certainly try to escape, but it was not possible.

I surveyed my surroundings, and for the first time, I was fully cognizant of where I was standing. All this time, I thought I understood what Hell was. But hearing what the angelic being said, I realized that this was not just the place for lost souls. Neither was it their final destination. Hell is a temporary holding place, God's maximum-security prison for those on spiritual death row. Hell is the Alcatraz of the spiritual realm, and no one will escape.

As a matter of fact, in Revelation 20:14, the Bible says that Hell shall be consumed:

"And death and hell were cast into the lake of fire. This is the second death."

When I realised what Hell was, I began to see the angels at the gate's entrance in a new light. They were prison wardens assigned by God to make sure that the rules and regulations set in place were obeyed. And the spirit beings, like the one that dragged the woman back down into the pit, were prisoners themselves. But because of their wickedness and undiluted hatred, they took on the role of sadistic prison guards to ensure that their fellow inmates suffered as much as them.

All this time on the tour, I thought I was only there to witness the horrors of Hell. But I was also being shown the legal processes of the Supreme Court of Heaven being carried out. The people I saw were not just the inhabitants of Hell. They were the accused who had been charged and found guilty and were now awaiting their final sentencing.

This was a supernatural penitentiary, and just as the angel had said, every prisoner knew precisely why they were there. A heightened consciousness of all they had done left them with inescapable culpability that was seared into their condemned hearts forever. The irony was that they were excruciatingly aware of all the wrong they had done but never able to repent. Overwhelming remorse is possible in Hell, but true repentance is not, so no one comes out even if they wanted to. They wouldn't even if they could and couldn't even if they would.

My head was spinning from the dizzying revelation I had just received. Scriptures rushed from my heart to my mind to confirm the understanding I was being given. And the gravity of what the angelic being said shook me to the core. As dreadful as Hell is, it is only a holding cell. This was just a trailer for the feature film, a foretaste of things to come. What was ahead would make the inhabitants of Hell wish they were back in Hell.

The countdown has begun. A day is coming when all of the inhabitants of Hell – and even Hell itself – will be cast into the lake of fire. Hell will be punished, and everything in it. It will be a day of final judgment where the searing hot liquid blue flames of Hell will seem like the good old days.

I saw too many horrors in Hell that would trouble the bravest of men. Even worms that no horror film could ever recreate on set. I will do my best to describe these in the next chapter.

Chapter 8

The Worms in Hell

The blood-curdling screams stopped me in my tracks. I whipped my head around to look towards the sound. It was coming from one of the pits. The sound grew louder and more intense, and amidst the screams, I could hear the unmistakable sound of teeth chattering.

I live in Britain, and I know what it's like to be so cold that you can hear your teeth chatter, but this was unlike anything I had ever heard before. This was not from the cold. This was from mind-numbing pain.

Pain on Earth is a noxious and powerful force. However, here there are things we can do to manage or even inhibit pain. No such mediums exist in Hell. The body you are given has the ability to feel pain, but there are no mechanisms to block or diminish that pain. There are no protective coverings or pain killers. The body, which is spiritual yet physical, is exposed like a raw nerve, with senses that are heightened to intensify whatever torture is inflicted upon it.

Pain on Earth can be more or less intense depending on the severity of the stimulus. No such measurement exists in Hell. The bottom of the pain scale in Hell starts at a level a million times beyond excruciating and increases from there. The stimuli are in abundance, and I was about to get a close-up look at one of them.

The Lord bent down and thrust His hand like a shovel into the ashy bottom of the pit. I could see his hand elongating like something out of a special effects film. But this was real. He scooped up some of the ash which had chunks of burning red and bluish coals. Within them were worms.

These worms are fireproof. They can withstand any level of heat Hell can dish out, tremendous heat. They can dart in and out of the liquid blue flame and devour the molten flesh of their target while the body is still on fire.

I know of species of worms on Earth that not only survive but thrive in the harshest and most volatile conditions. Some are accomplished hunters and creatures so intense that they live in conditions that would incinerate most other creatures. They make their homes on the lip of a volcano's edge, preferring to get as close to the searing heat as possible. They are predatory champions, tough as nails, and have managed to survive mass extinctions. Poisonous spines covering their bodies kill anything that tries to eat them, making them virtually untouchable. However extraordinary the earthly species are, they are nothing compared to their relatives in Hell.

The things of Earth are a mere shadow of what exists in Heaven. The things I've seen in Heaven are much more real and beautiful in their perfection than their earthly counterparts. On my tour of Hell, I discovered that Earth also shadows what exists in Hell. Moreover, in Hell, they are perfected in hideousness and gross aberrations. One such example is the worms.

I leaned forward to get a closer look at what the Lord was showing me. These were no ordinary looking worms. They were cognizant. Now, I must pause to explain that worms on Earth are not the mindless creatures they appear to be. One study carried out by scientists found that worms would sometimes think for themselves. If worms on Earth could be found to have such faculties, that only gives you a hint of what the worms in Hell were capable of. The study went on to suggest that worms, like human beings, have a sense of free will.

Just looking at the worms of Hell, I could see that they had understanding and wisdom and knowledge. They were cognizant of the people, why they were there, and Hell itself. They had a deeper knowledge of that place and anything that could come there. And what's more, they could choose what they wanted to do to their prey and how.

I looked at the Lord, wondering why He was showing me these creatures. What might they be for?

He answered my thoughts. "Have you not read what I said in My word. There will be gnashing of teeth where their worm dieth not."

The worms of Hell do not die – they cannot – neither do they have respect for the living dead. On Earth, most worms will at least have the decency to wait until you are a corpse before they try to devour your flesh, but Hell has no such courtesies. These carnivorous creatures burrow through the flesh-like bodies of the condemned of their own volition, fully aware of what they are doing and the effect their torment is having.

No scale can measure the intensity of the pain inflicted on the victim of these carnivorous creatures. With every piercing movement of the worms, the host let out a bone-chilling scream. It was as though the sheaths of every nerve in their supernatural bodies were being peeled away. And at the same time, a billion razor-sharp incisors were gnawing at the exposed nerves inside. Hell is no petting zoo, and these are only a few of the creatures that are there.

I understood, with esoteric knowledge, the meaning of "gnashing of teeth." I heard for myself the sound of teeth crashing against teeth and the noisy clatter of bones shaking of people wracked with unimaginable pain.

"Come up higher."

The Lord's voice cut through the haze of noise and pain. And as if we were flying, we arrived at the exact spot where I had heard the sound, and I could see people in fear, losing themselves in pain.

There was lightning in the Lord's eyes when He spoke. "Warn My people. I do not want to see them here. I died for them so they wouldn't come here. This place was not created for them. It was meant for the devil and his angels, not mankind."

Rapists, murderers, thieves, robbers, other-worldly tormentors, and worms are not the only ones that make up the hosts of Hell. It is a place where you are confined and isolated, but at the same time, there are things that can access you at any time in the terrifying darkness. In Hell, your spiritual eyes are opened, not to see in the dark, but to see every frightening apparition that emerges from the dark blackness. On the next stop of the tour, I saw two of these sights. One of them, you would desire ardently to see on

Earth, but you would rather have your eyes gouged out than to see it in Hell. The other you see in Hell but are blind to it on Earth.

Chapter 9

The Hallucinations in Hell

Hell is a merchant of fake hope. First, an unforeseen force presents the thing one wishes to happen – with all the toppings – as if in a hallucinogenic form. Then, just as one feels they are about to see the fruition of that hope, it is snatched away as soon as it arrives.

In one of the many scenes I saw, I vividly recall this one man. He seemed middle-aged to me. He was presented with such false hope, only for it to be taken away abruptly before he could embrace it. It seems these hallucinogenic moments were ushered in to alter the awareness of his surroundings as well as his own thoughts and feelings, causing him sensations and bringing images that seemed real though they were not. Additionally, dissociative impulses were added to him from an unforeseen source. These impulses caused him to feel out of control or disconnected from his body and environment, yet still connected to the pain prescribed for him.

The man appeared to be sitting in a cell, which was pitch black, blacker than Vantablack, the darkest material created on earth. Vantablack absorbs up to 99.965% of visible light. But in this cell, there was no visible light whatsoever. The inhabitant was grinding his teeth in anticipation of the next tortuous encounter. He knew it was coming. It always did. But what would it be this time?

You see, in Hell, the terror is always fresh in the mind of the victim. There is no ability to brace yourself for the expected. The mind can no longer prepare itself in that way. You just knew something dreadful is about to happen. Part of the terror by design is not knowing what it will be. And even if it were a repeat experience, it would terrify you as if happening for the very first time.

He turned his head right to left frantically, over and over, not even really being sure he was looking in the direction he thought. He could see nothing. He could sense nothing but his own fear. The groans and the wailing cries of countless other tormented souls were amplified and seemed to be coming from everywhere, all at once. Suddenly, the cell becomes deathly silent. His mind begins to race. *What is happening?* Stepping out of the darkness, the most beautiful woman appears and seems to illuminate the area directly in front of him. *What's going on? Could it be the torment is finally over?*

There she stands before him, a quintessential beauty in face and form. His eyes widen in disbelief. *How did she get in here?* But there she was, flawless, an exquisite representation of everything a man could desire. He is lost in a timeless moment, appraising her and drinking in this other-worldly beauty. She is a feast for his eyes.

He was so far removed from reality as he once knew it, he wasn't sure if he was hallucinating or if she was really there. *Maybe if I could just touch her.*

He inches forward tentatively, slowly, and painstakingly shuffling one foot forward then the next. His eyes are fastened on hers, which are deep and alluring. She smiles as now he is close enough to touch her. He feels compelled to be as close to her as possible. And then it happens.

Her eyes that seemed to beckon him moments before turned blood red and then as black as the pitch darkness he was accustomed to. Then, as if a million snakes lying dormant beneath the surface suddenly awakened, her skin begins to crawl and ripple, tearing and folding as the texture morphs into something grotesque and alien. The once delicate and slender fingers are now gnarled with dagger-like claws. The mouth that had looked like it was ready to drip words like honey had peeled back to reveal multiple layers of black and blood-stained fangs. It was cavernous and filled with all that represented death and malevolence. It was hideous beyond description, infinitely worse than anything you could imagine from the darkest horror movie. And it was millimetres away from his face.

Torture is any act by which severe pain or suffering, whether physical or mental, is intentionally inflicted on a person. There are many methods of psychological torture on Earth. One form of torture happens when a person is exposed to enduring and repeated aversive stimuli beyond their control. Imagine the effect on the mind when you realize there will never be an end to the grotesque sights and heinous activities to which you will be exposed. It produces a sense of utter powerlessness. Other techniques include sleep deprivation and sensory deprivation, being confined to a dark place, for example. On Earth, each of these forms of psychological torture can cause permanent brain damage. The victim becomes mentally disturbed.

There are many other forms of psychological torture on Earth. As dreadful as they all are, Hell is infinitely worse. The various methods of psychological torture enacted on its inhabitants are maniacal and strategic. They are fine-tuned, heightened, and executed with maximum efficiency. I witnessed first-hand one of the most horrendous forms of psychological torment using one of the things we desire on Earth the most, beauty.

There are spirit beings in Hell, grotesque, distorted creatures that defy description. You would expect to see such beings in Hell. They are spawned of all that is evil, foul, monstrous, and hideous. Now, imagine having such creatures suddenly appear out of the blackness millimetres from your face. That would be horrifying enough, but that is just the start of this particular form of psychological torture.

This was not my first time seeing something like this. I have seen countless visions of Heaven, Hell, angels, demons, departed saints, creatures before the throne, and many more. So I knew demons can have a front.

Hell has a way of presenting the thing you would desire the most and turning it into something that you would find the most terrifying and repulsive. Such was the case with these spirit beings. They appear before you in the blackness, but initially, they are not in their true form. They transform themselves into the most beautiful beings.

The kind of beauty I saw is beyond anything I've ever seen on Earth in any beauty pageant or modelling agency. It's beyond anything you would consider strikingly beautiful or handsome or stunning both in face and figure. In that instant, the victim thinks they are resting their eyes on something beautiful. The very next second, the spirit being unveils itself, piercing their eyes with its hideous appearance. Hell epitomizes the saying, "all that glitters is not gold." Beauty exists in Hell but only to be used as an instrument of terror.

I remembered a scripture in 2 Corinthians 11:14:

"And no marvel; for Satan himself is transformed into an angel of light."

The Unfortunate Pain in Hell

The unfortunate thing about Hell is that the inhabitants have no ability to "catch on." There is never a moment where they would be able to brace themselves for what will inevitably happen. There is no learning mode in Hell, so every time something horrific happens, it's as though it's happening for the very first time. Terror is always freshly served. It's like the woman who tried to escape from the pit only to have a spirit being mutilate her body and drag her back down just when she thought freedom was within her reach. Hell creates desire and then delivers devasting disappointment.

In Hell, you are allowed to have visitors. Spirit beings can access your cell without your permission, and they are not the only ones. Other visitors come. These have mouths, but they do not speak. They come hungry, but they are never filled. Not only do they invade the occupant's cell, but also their body. They are the worms. These were different from the ones the Lord had shown me earlier.

The worms I saw this time were reddish; some were silvery-white like platinum, others were like a mixture of white, silver, and black. Now, when I speak of worms, you might be thinking of something the size of a typical earthworm. No, they are not small like that. Right now, there are worms on Earth that grow up to 3 meters (10 feet) long. Some can reach a length of as much as 7 meters (22 feet) and can weigh over 1.5 kilograms (over 3 pounds). One exceptionally large worm specimen found in the foothills of the Sumaco Volcano in Ecuador is the diameter of a man's wrist. The worms I saw in Hell were of this magnitude, about the diameter of my forearm.

When a person dies on Earth, worms eat the flesh. That's what worms do; they eat dead or decaying organic matter. That is why they are called decomposers. It should be no surprise that there are worms in Hell since it is filled with rotting flesh. On Earth, the human body is filled with bacteria. These microorganisms aid us in digestion and help to keep harmful bacteria at a minimum. However, when the body dies, these bacteria start to feed on their host and break the body down from the inside out.

After the corpse is buried for a long time, worms in the ground penetrate the casket and the decomposed flesh by burrowing, as they are apt to do. But these are not earthworms. While they bear a slight resemblance to the most enormous earthworms in size and function, that is where the similarity ends. These are not worms of Earth; these are worms of Hell.

I saw these gigantic worms eating the flesh of Hell's inhabitants. They eat and are never satisfied. They eat until the flesh is consumed, and then they start all over again. They never finish. As I looked on, the Lord again answered my thoughts before I could articulate them.

"Even if they touch one and try to kill it, they can't."

I watched people sobbing in agony, but they cried to no avail. Nothing changed or will ever change. It was a sorrowful sight. I turned to the Lord.

"Lord, how long will they be here?" I will never forget His answer.

"Have you not read My words? This is a place where their worm dieth not, and the fire is not quenched. I said there will be gnashing of teeth forever and ever."

I called to remembrance Mark 9:43-48:

"And if thy hand offend thee, cut it off: it is better for thee to enter into life maimed, than having two hands to go into hell, into the fire that never shall be quenched: Where their worm dieth not, and the fire is not quenched. And if thy foot offend thee, cut it off: it is better for thee to enter halt into life, than having two feet to be cast into hell, into the fire that never shall be quenched: Where their worm dieth not, and the fire is not quenched. And if thine eye offend thee, pluck it out: it is better for thee to enter into the kingdom of God with one eye, than having two eyes to be cast into hell fire: Where their worm dieth not, and the fire is not quenched."

And also Luke 13:28:

"There shall be weeping and gnashing of teeth, when ye shall see Abraham, and Isaac, and Jacob, and all the

prophets, in the kingdom of God, and you yourselves thrust out."

Bear in mind, the torments of Hell are not polite or mutually exclusive. They do not wait in turn so that when one stops the other starts. No. You experience levels and dimensions of various kinds of pain and suffering at the same time. Your flesh is rotting and being eaten by worms. At the same time, this rotting worm-eaten flesh is burning. Such is the nature of Hell, a barrage of the most excruciating torment imaginable.

Everything I am describing here is not something that will happen in the future. These things are taking place right now in Hell. The worms are feasting; the fires are burning; there is gnashing of teeth. Someone joked and said, "What about those of us who don't have teeth?" If you do not have teeth, you will be given teeth so that you can gnash those teeth. Hell is no laughing matter. This is a harsh reality this next group of people I'm about to tell you about sadly discovered. And this one hit home.

Chapter 10

Whosoever Will

Hell is a gallery of inexpressible horrors. From one exhibit to the next, the sights and sounds, the very atmosphere, affects you in a way that changes everything about how you view life and death. Of all the painful scenes I witnessed in Hell, there is one that was most tragic.

There was a man who was also visiting Hell. He was also moving from one painful exhibit to the next. He also had the burden of witnessing the atrocities of Hell inflicted on the people. But the most touching and heartbreaking scene was when we came to a cell in a certain region of Hell and saw the man's family in torment. That man was the Lord Himself, and the people He saw were His own sons and daughters.

God is not a terrorist. He does not employ fear tactics, nor does He manipulate your will to persuade you to choose Heaven over Hell. The choice is yours. Love is the only means God uses to draw you to Himself. I am simply here as a messenger to tell you what I saw when I was taken beyond the curtain of time to a place called Hell.

I did not want to go there, but I was taken there so that I could relate what I saw so that you also will not want to go there. Hell was never made for you. It was made for the devil and his angels, not human beings. I know that there are people who choose to go to Hell, but I was surprised to see so many of these.

The Lord showed me a place in Hell where self-righteous Christians were.

He sighed. "This is a place of pride." He paused for a moment before continuing as if the words had taken something out of Him. "Self-righteousness is pride."

I could hardly believe what I was seeing. There, in this region of Hell reserved for prideful people, were many pastors. Some of them were well-known founders of churches. Even now, we have people name themselves as spiritual sons of these men of God, yet there they were, burning in Hell. I want you to understand that these were not sinners. The people I was allowed by God to see were Christians, some of the big names in the Kingdom, and they are weeping there in Hell.

Most of the pastors I saw were the offended, people who came out of other people's churches in the wrong way. Some of them were crying out to the Lord about the watered-down messages they had preached. Some had compromised the Gospel and put the people they were supposed to be leading at risk just so they could maintain a certain image. Some were crying for not treating another pastor right. Some had misused church money. Some were in adulterous relationships. I saw bishops, popes, popular evangelists, popular teachers, popular prophets, world-renowned Apostles, and preachers of the Gospel. They were all burning.

There was even a place in Hell where I saw pastors who had fought other pastors. In fact, one of them had been collecting information about other pastors to keep and use as ammunition just in case other pastors fought against him. Pastors, preachers, deacons, elders – they all make up a large population of Hell.

As the Lord and I plod on wearily, we walked by a certain man of God. He shouted when he saw us.

"I used to heal. I used to pray for people. I used to preach the Gospel."

The Lord stopped and turned towards the man. He was not angry, but His voice was forceful yet sombre. "No, you were not healing. When you stood in front of the church, I healed My people out of mercy and benevolence, out of charity. And you kept on doing wrong things, thinking I was approving of what you were doing. No, I saw the pain in My people, and you were deceiving them. So, I healed them."

These people could see the Lord, and the moment they saw Him, they began to cry out. "Lord, help me! I could have changed, but it was because ..." And from there they would make excuses and start blaming other people for their misfortune. It is one of the most piteous scenes I have ever witnessed. They were sobbing as they cried out to the Lord. But the worst part was the finality of the Lord's sorrowful response.

"Judgment was set. It's a judgment that was set before the ages of the world, and judgment was set before We began the world. You were given many opportunities to repent, but you did not repent."

These were pastors, apostles, evangelists, prophets, teachers, and preachers crying out to the Lord. They sounded so sincere, but as soon as they heard His response, they began to curse Him. That was proof that they were crying out only because they wanted to escape their pain, not because they really believed He is the Lord. You know, there is something about seeing Jesus walking by, knowing He's the only One who can save you, and realizing no deliverance will ever take place.

The Lord turned to me. "Son, this is what happens continuously. These people want out, but it's not possible for them to repent."

"Not possible for them to repent?" The Lord's words struck my heart like shards of glass, and I struggled to accept what He was saying. "Lord, You say You love Your people. How come when they cry out in Hell You cannot forgive them?"

He looked at me with tears in His eyes. "Son, go and tell My people."

Then I understood that as painful as it was for me to hear those words, it was immeasurably more painful for Him to say them and to accept the finality of their fate.

Jesus died here on Earth. Salvation is only possible here on Earth, and no one is completely changed until they receive Christ. Since they did not receive Christ here on Earth, there is no power in them to repent. To fully repent, you need Christ. Once you're in Hell, there is no way to repent, no way. If you need Christ, you must receive Him on Earth, not in Hell.

Children and Hell

One thing that I saw, or I should say, did not see were children. Although Hell has been the muse of many Hollywood movies, a tour of Hell trumps anything you would see on a cinema screen. Some of you may have seen films with children acting roles where they are Satanists. But I can tell you with certainty because I was there, I did not see any children in Hell, not one. Children were not the only thing that was absent from Hell. Something else was missing.

In Hell, time is absent. It is a place where there is no hope of relief; there is no end to suffering because time is not present. How can suffering end if there is no end? It is difficult to explain the absence of time. But imagine, for a moment, that you are in excruciating pain, and you know relief will come at 2 o'clock on the dot. You look at the clock, and it is 1:59, and the second hand is on 59 seconds. One more second, and it will be 2 o'clock.

The second hand quivers, but it never moves. The hands of time are broken beyond repair, and time has stopped. Relief never comes. Torment never ends. Instead of you watching time, time watches you with mocking eyes, remembering when you mocked time on Earth.

Hear these things I saw "twice." Take this writing to heart. We'll go over them in summary.

Chapter 11

A Recap of Hell

"Hell is a living organism. It is something with a belly, with legs, with a head, with walls, and even with jaws."

As I continued my tour of Hell, the Lord's words were echoing in my mind. I thought Hell would be one big pit with millions upon millions of people all being tormented in one location. But it was not like that at all. This was a revelation that I received while I was in Hell that I could not have understood as I do now without that visitation.

You see, Hell is an architectural and geological supernatural phenomenon. It has a carefully designed structure. There is nothing random or haphazard about it. All the places I saw were laid out in a particular way. It is well organized. Just as the planets in Earth's solar system are all fixed at specific distances and held in place so that they do not collide or intersect, every place in Hell is perfectly positioned for its designed purpose.

The terrain of Hell is not just one massive pit, as depicted in some paintings. It has its own unique topography. Hell is vast and varied. It has levels, cells, and compartments. And there are regions in Hell, zones, some great distances from others. All of Hell is not created equal. And as I contemplated what the Lord said, I began to understand that Hell was not only an architectural and geological marvel. What the Lord said revealed that it was also a biological wonder.

You see, this was more than a walking tour of a geographical location. I was experiencing an endoscopic view of the internal anatomy of a living organism called Hell. The Lord's words dawned upon my mind, and I glanced back at the gates where I had entered. It was then I realized that if Hell has a head, the place where I had entered, that I had recognized before only as gates, were, in fact, the jaws of Hell.

It was a disturbing revelation, and my mind tried to draw a correlation between what I was seeing and what I had seen. I thought about the human jaw and its ability to exert as much as 125 kilograms – nearly 276 pounds – of pressure. That is more than the weight of a giant panda or a newborn elephant. The only reason we do not bite harder than we do is that our teeth do not have the capability to withstand the pressure of biting down that hard. I found myself grinding my own teeth slightly at the very thought of the jaws of Hell.

Then I remembered seeing news footage on Earth of the hydraulic tool that is used on cars involved in the worst and most fatal accidents. It earned the nickname the Jaws of Life because it can apply immense pressure to rescue a person from the wreckage, and ultimately from the jaws of death. The imagery of the idiom is that of a wild animal that uses its powerful jaws to trap, then kill, its prey.

Again, I looked at the gates of Hell, deceptively coated in white, like teeth, but dark black within, like a gigantic rotten cavity. I began to understand the monstrosity that it is. On

Earth, the Jaws of life rescue the trapped from certain death. But the jaws of Hell, like a ravening wild beast, are designed to trap, with incalculable pressure, the dead who could never be rescued. You enter to be masticated, swallowed, then regurgitated, only to be crushed all over again. There is no escape except for one brief moment in a timeless eternity when the inhabitants of Hell will be vomited up to face their final judgment.

Not only does Hell have jaws, but it also has a belly. It gets hungry and welcomes the lost with the growl of an enormous voracious beast that can never be satisfied. It demands the presence of the wicked as if by right. It feasts on a diet of wickedness, pain, and suffering. It is a cannibalistic living organism that consumes the flesh of its own kind, which is pure unadulterated evil. It has a head with jaws, and it has a belly, but it does not have arms because once you are inside, there is only one direction you can go, and that's down. However, as the Lord pointed out, it has legs.

Hell has legs, but it does not walk. It has legs for now and later. One day, those legs will bow to the One to whom Hell must answer in judgment. But now, as I moved down through Hell, I began to understand what the Lord said in a different way. At first, I heard it as, "It is something with a belly, with legs, with a head, with jaws." But after touring Hell, I understood it as "something with a belly with legs, with a head with jaws." Hell has levels, extremities. It ranges from low to lowest. The head, with its devastating jaws, is the apex of where the punishment begins. The legs are the extremities of Hell, the furthest point where the punishment is the most extreme. But even in Hell, the Lord shows mercy.

Imagine being cast into prison because you stole from someone. But instead of being placed in a regular cell, you were thrust into the worst solitary confinement with the vilest and most sadistic deviants known to man. There were no rules and no limitations or restrictions to what they could do to you. They were allowed to do whatever their blackened hearts desired. Would that be merciful?

In Hell, you are not casually tossed in wherever there is a vacancy or with whomever for a cellmate. No. Every inhabitant of Hell is assigned to a level and a personal compartment befitting the degree of their wickedness. Everyone is not punished in the same way or to the same degree. God could have categorically punished all the wicked in the same way. But even in punishment, He is merciful to mankind.

You might be wondering, *how is that merciful since everyone in Hell is suffering?* Well, there is something else I learnt about Hell. Yes, everyone is suffering there, sadly by their own choice. But the intensity of the torment is not the same for everyone. I told you about the people I saw being consumed repeatedly by the liquid blue flame. What I did not tell you before is that Hell has varying degrees of heat. Just as the human body has varying temperatures in different parts, each zone in Hell has its own thermostat, and there are differences in heat.

The fires of Hell burn differently in different places of the organism. What makes them burn differently? Nobody knows. But there are regions in Hell that are hotter than in other areas. It is not that if you were permitted to go to the less hot parts, you would feel comfortable. No, not at all. There is no comfortable place in Hell, only hot and hotter. Unlike the human body that is hotter nearest the upper parts, Hell is hotter at the lowest extremities – the legs.

Another proof of the mercy of God in Hell is that the devil is not there. If you found it difficult to imagine a thief imprisoned in the same cell as sadistic blood-thirsty monsters, just imagine what it would be like if the devil could have his way in Hell right now. I assure you, he is not there, but one day, he will be. He will never have his way in Hell. Of all the captives, he will be the most tormented, just as the Lord reminded me.

"Have you not read that he shall be brought down to Hell, to the sides of the pit?"

There is a dungeon in the uttermost extremity of Hell with the devil's name on it. In the anatomy of Hell, the sides of the pit refer to the extreme parts of Hell, the lowest, hottest part, the place of the most severe torment. That is where the devil will be positioned. He *shall* be brought down to Hell. He is not there yet, but he does not have any say in the matter.

Hell is a place of torment, misery, and punishment for evil, where one becomes fully aware of one's negative actions but cannot make any amends. It is the place or state where the bodies and souls of the inhabitants are consumed by unquenchable fires of varying degrees. You are trapped, constantly under attack, like a foreign entity in a hellish immune system.

I was not permitted to see every part of Hell because there are regions where no visitation is allowed. Just like in a penitentiary where the worst and most savage criminals are imprisoned in isolated areas away from other prisoners, Hell also has its own visitation restrictions. Right now, there are prohibited regions of solitary confinement where only the most fiendish and nefarious beings are held captive.

I saw many things in Hell, sights I cannot forget. And I visited various areas of Hell. But there was one thing that I did not see that may come as a surprise to you. I did not see a single demon in Hell. As I said before, they are not there. There are spiritual beings, but no demons are in Hell. However, there are fallen angels which are isolated in a region of Hell where no one is permitted to enter. There they will remain, fastened in chains in the deepest, darkest dungeons of Hell, until a time of judgment.

"For Hell shall be thrown into the lake of fire. Have you not wondered why Hell should be punished?"

The question the Lord asked me earlier came flooding back to my mind. It is difficult to explain. However, you must understand that there is a physicality in the spiritual world that is not the physicality of the natural world. Hell is spiritual, but it is also physical. You can experience physical pain in a body that is spiritual. You can experience differences in heat. But the inhabitants are not the only ones that can feel pain. Hell can also feel.

God will punish Hell because it is a living organism. It is not an inanimate physical location. It is alive. It has senses. It has an appetite. It is not just a holding cell for those in torment; it also inflicts it. And for that, it will be punished in a place that burns infinitely hotter than the hottest fires in the lowest parts of Hell.

The Lord was with me during my tour of Hell. I was grateful for that because I did not want to be there. No one would wish to see the things that I saw. But as I turned to the Lord, I realized that His desire to not see the horrors of Hell was infinitely greater than mine. He did not want to be there either. What's more, He did not want to see any human being in Hell.

I remember looking at His face, and He was sobbing.

"Do you see all these people, son? I love them. If only they had chosen Me at the time that is set for them to choose Me."

You need to understand that Hell was never intended for you or for any human being. God created Hell for the devil and his fallen angels. Through hot tears, the Lord surveyed the damnable sights once more. He was inconsolable, experiencing the conflict of a God of mercy whose hands had been tied. A feeling of utter helplessness washed over me. Seeing the Lord whom I loved so much weeping twisted my insides, and I too wept.

Chapter 12

The End of The First Tour

The Lord pointed toward the gates near where we had entered. "Look."

At first, I tried to see what it was. Everything looked the same as before, nothing different. I kept looking, but I did not know what I was supposed to be seeing.

Then the Lord said, "Come up hither."

I immediately moved towards him, but I was not walking. When He commanded me to come up, I just arrived where He was.

Instantly, we were in a certain location. Then the Lord pointed his right index finger and used it to draw a line in the air, a vertical line, from top to bottom, as if cutting a slit in a seamless curtain. The angel who stood by put his hand through the opening and stretched one side to the other side, as if there was about to be a grand reveal. What I saw defies human comprehension.

Through the opening, something like a cloud appeared. However, this was no ordinary cloud. It seemed to be some sort of ultra-dimensional visualizer or screen, as it were. There really is nothing on Earth that I can truly liken the experience to. The closest I can think of would be like looking through a pair of virtual or augmented reality glasses that were bigger than an IMAX screen. But this was not virtual or augmented reality. This was real and beyond any human or earthly technology.

What I was seeing was superior to anything three-dimensional or even four-dimensional. It surpassed the dimensions of length, width, height, and time. It was beyond anything I can communicate in human terms. But for the sake of this writing, I will simply refer to it as 7000D.

As I looked into this 7000D cloud-like screen, I began to see events that were happening on the Earth. It was like zooming in from a crystal-clear satellite view. However, this was not a replication of what was there. I was there, literally, seeing everything that was happening there in real time.

I saw my brother in the house where he was staying in Britain. And as I continued looking, another scene began to unfold right before my eyes. I shifted my attention from where my brother was inside the house to something else that was happening. There, loitering outside his house, were evil spirits. They were on assignment, intending to take my brother's life. And then the Lord spoke.

"Look at him."

I looked again at my brother. He was totally unaware of what was happening right outside his house. My heart quickened its pace as I watched the menacing scene playing out on Earth. I had a birds-eye view of what was taking place, yet, at the same time, I was right there. All of a sudden, my brother stood up and began to pace in the house. He prayed a little bit, and then sat down. I kept looking, trying to figure out what was happening or about to happen. Then the angel said something that left me bewildered.

"If he does not repent, he will become ..."

I waited, thinking perhaps he might add more to what he said. *Become what?* But the angel remained quiet.

Then the Lord pointed away from that 7000D cloud, and the scene changed. I saw an area in Hell close to where I had entered the gates. As I followed the direction of His finger, my eyes were drawn to two massive green trees. They stood out from the charred terrain because they were green. But they were withered. It struck me as odd that these trees were green, suggesting the presence of life, yet withered as if they were already dead. What was even more peculiar was that the tree had fruit on it. Typically, on Earth, you would not see a dried-up tree producing fruit. But this was not Earth; this was Hell.

The shrivelled limbs were laden with fruit, and each piece was arranged to form letters of a word. The words were huge and seemed to be inscribed on the boughs. It was as if I was looking at a billboard made of some kind of spiritually organic material that no one could ignore. It was in Hell, yes, but still a sight to behold. I marvelled though I was conscious of the surrounding stench and cries of those in pain.

I remember staring at the words, wondering what beauty could be found here and why this little place gave a sense of eerie hope. I was really confused because they were not written in a language I understood. Additionally, the fruits were green, which was a pure anomaly when everything else I saw in that small part of that location of Hell was either dying or dead.

On one tree, the word looked like AUDIOM. And on the next tree was written a certain word I cannot disclose here. I was troubled, struggling to understand this seemingly encrypted message. *What does this strange two-worded statement mean?*

The Lord said, "I will explain to you by revelation what this means."

I was relieved to hear the Lord had plans to explain what the words meant. However, I did not know what He meant when He said He would explain it "by revelation." It would not be until after the visitation ended that I would come to understand what He meant.

You see, this visitation happened while I was studying at Salford University to get my first degree in finance. My wife was a semester behind me studying for the same degree. After the visitation ended, with the words still fresh in my mind, I told my wife what I'd seen, and we immediately rushed out the door and drove straight to the university library. We scoured the Internet. We searched dictionaries. We searched everything we could find to try to discover what those words meant. But we could not find them anywhere. We headed back home, and as I walked through the front door, something caught my eye. There on the shelf was an old etymological dictionary. I did not have much hope that I would find anything in it after our exhaustive searches at the university, but I figured it was worth a try.

I flipped through the pages, half expecting to reach another disappointing dead end. Au ... Aud ... My finger travelled down the page and stopped. There, on the page in crisp black text, was the word I was searching for. After writing down the meaning I had found, I quickly flipped to another section in search of the second word. It was there too. The message I had seen spelt out in the trees near the gateway of Hell had been written in what is commonly known as the blueprint of languages, Latin. The words combined formed the word *reprobate,* which means to be cut off from the salvation of God. It was then that I understood the revelation and why the Lord had looked at me the way He did as He pointed to the words on the withered trees.

"He will become." The words He had spoken about my brother were reverberating in my very being. There was an urgency in the Lord's eyes. They flashed with a strange and frightening mixture of raw power, like lightning, and seriousness intermingled with sorrow. I could see tears in the Lord's eyes, and I could feel them. The message the Lord had taken such great pains to show me was clear and compelling. He was telling me that if my brother did not repent, he would be cut off from the salvation of God, and he would come to this dreadful place called Hell.

The sight of the tormented souls in Hell was enough incentive for me to warn anybody not to go there. But this was something else. This motivated me on another level; this was personal. This was my brother. I knew I needed to do something, and there was no time to be wasted. I had one goal and one desire burning in my heart, and that was to get him to repent.

I drove straight to my brother's house to talk to him. As we sat down and I began to talk to him about his life and the state of his soul, it occurred to me that there was something quite familiar about what was happening, almost like déjà vu. It was as though I was acting out a script. Then I remembered, I had seen this scene before. It was on the 7000D screen. I recalled watching and at the same time seeing myself talking to him and getting him to repent. But that was not all I saw.

In that same vision on the 7000D screen, after I talked to my brother, I saw a river appear in front of him. It was more like a swamp. The water looked stagnant and murky, brownish-green in colour and was covered with green marsh foam. There was no way to tell what lay beneath the opaque surface. I watched as he stood on the bank looking at the water. Then, much to my surprise, he got in. I did not understand what I was seeing. *I've already spoken to him and gotten him to repent. What is happening now?*

The Lord said, "Look."

So I looked, and I saw myself there with my brother giving him instructions. In the vision, I was also holding some baskets. Then the Lord spoke to me within the vision.

"Put the baskets down."

I saw myself in the 7000D screen putting the baskets down. Then my brother waded further into the swamp and started to fish. He reached down under the murky water and began to bring out fish by the handfuls. There were all kinds of fish, a lot of them, and as he fished them out of the water, he put them into the baskets which I had set on the ground.

I noticed something else about his strange catch. As he filled up the baskets, I could see that the fish had snails biting their mouths. *Why are the snails biting the mouths of the fish?* I had never seen or heard of anything like that before. Also, I could see that some of the fish were covered with parasites, and I could tell by the scales of some of them that they were diseased. Others had severe deformities. I watched intently, but I could not make sense of what I was seeing.

Then the Lord interrupted my thoughts. "Do you see? He shall be what he is doing right now. What he is doing right now is what he shall be."

I turned to the Lord, still perplexed. Then, when He remained quiet, I turned to the angel who responded.

"He shall be a great evangelist."

My eyes widened, and the angel continued. "If you look at the fish, it shall be any type of thing, especially people that are really, really lost and think they are not accepted. He shall bring them to Christ. He shall bring them to Christ."

I turned to look at my brother again, now through the eyes of this new revelation. The look of excitement on his face as he continued catching fish made my heart leap with joy.

Then the Lord, who had also been watching my brother, turned to me again. "Go back, and tell My people that I'm coming soon."

In a flash, as He continued, I remembered all I had seen in Hell. "They do not need to be in this location. Tell your brother to change. Tell your brother to receive Me. It is My free gift. And tell the world I'm coming very soon! I'm coming very soon! I'm coming very soon!"

The emphatic repetition and sternness in His voice shook me to the core.

"I'm coming very soon. They don't need to be in this place. I'm coming very soon!"

Chapter 13

Never Forget

This book is your Mansfield bar. It is a warning. I went to Hell, and I will never forget what I saw. I will never forget the alarming and speedy descent into the core of the earth. I will never forget Hell's vast gates swinging open to swallow its masses. I will never forget the sand dunes that were scorched from the inferno raging beneath, the outer cavity of a burning furnace. I could never forget the suffocating putrid stench of Hell, nor the terrorizing blanket of blackness filled with horrifying terrors that tormented the mind and the body. Never will I forget the suffocating atmosphere of Hell, where you gasp for air that does not exist, and wish for death only to remain on the verge of dying.

Emblazoned on my mind are the heinous acts of rape, murder, and every other violent act that the inhabitants were forced to endure over and over. I will never forget the woman who was brought to the brink of escape only to be dragged back down into the dark pit. I cannot forget the personalized fire that slowly incinerated the flesh from the soles of the person's feet to the crown of their head in a never-ending cycle. The psychological torment of the chameleon spirt beings that used beauty as an instrument of torture; the groanings and cries of Hell's captives whose suffering never ends – these things cannot be forgotten.

How could I ever forget the prideful Christians, pastors and congregants alike, who failed to take their salvation seriously because they never thought they would end up in Hell, or the utter loneliness and despair of being in a place where their worm never dies, the fire is never quenched, and time is no more. Above all, I will never forget that Hell is a place where your eyes are opened to see your Deliverer, but you can never be delivered because you can never, ever repent.

Take it from someone who has been there; you do not want to go to Hell. Although I was shown only a small part of it that I could contain, that small part I saw is enough to make you say I do not want to go to Hell. It's not necessary. There are more than 32,000 verses, sixty-six books of the Bible just so you won't go to Hell.

Remember the Lord's words, "The moment you did not choose Me on Earth, you decided that your desire is for Hell." If you make that choice, you leave the Lord no other option but to fulfil that desire. Hell is a crowded place. At the same time, it is a very lonely place. There is no time off or reduced sentences for good behaviour, no parole, no early release. Once you are there, you're there forever. Hell is real and you don't want to end up there!

Hell is inescapable, but not for you. The fact that you are reading this means you still have time to accept God's invitation and reject Hell's invitation. God loves you. He sent His Son, Jesus, to die for your sins so that you can be with Him for eternity. Choosing Heaven is simple. Are you ready to trust Jesus Christ as your Saviour and Lord or to rededicate your life to Christ? Make Jesus Christ the Lord of your life by praying this prayer now:

O Lord God, I come to You in the Name of Jesus Christ. I believe with all my heart in Jesus Christ, the Son of the living God. I believe He died for me, and God raised Him from the dead. I believe He's alive today and that He wants me to be with Him in Heaven. I confess with my mouth that Jesus Christ is the Lord of my life from this day. Through Him and in His Name, I have eternal life. I am born again. Thank you, Lord, for saving my soul! I'm now a child of God. Halleluiah!"

Congratulations! If you prayed that prayer, I want to celebrate with you and help nurture you in your new life in Christ. Send us an email at:

https://www.uebertangel.org/contact.

Let us know that you read this book, *I Went to Hell*, and what Bible church or Christian community you have joined. We want to celebrate with you knowing that Heaven is now your home.